# LOW INCOME SAVINGS CHALLENGES

# Money bingo

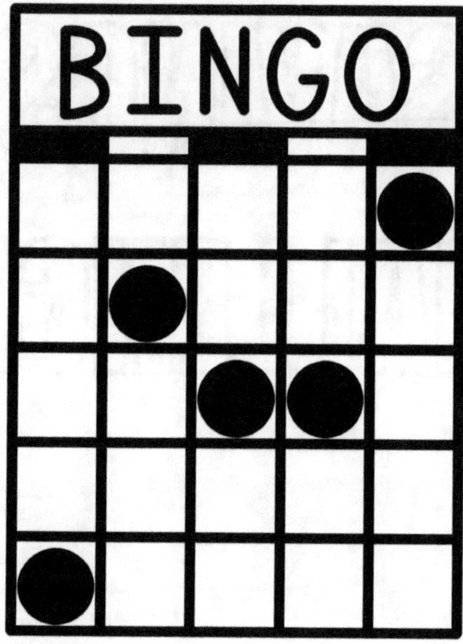


Money bingo is a flexible savings approach, the idea being you have dollar amounts on your bingo board which you cross off as you save them in no particular order. When your bingo card is full, you have saved the amount stated at the top of the card. There is a start and end date on each card so you can set the time frame.

# Money Bingo $100

Start:          End:

| | | | | | | | | |
|---|---|---|---|---|---|---|---|---|
| $4 |  | $3 |  | $1 |  |  | $1 |  |
|  |  | $1 | $5 |  |  |  |  | $2 |
|  | $2 |  |  | $2 | $2 |  |  |  |

| | | | | | | | | |
|---|---|---|---|---|---|---|---|---|
|  |  |  | $3 | $1 |  |  |  | $5 |
| $2 |  | $4 |  |  |  |  | $1 |  |
|  |  |  | $1 |  |  | $1 | $2 |  |

| | | | | | | | | |
|---|---|---|---|---|---|---|---|---|
|  | $3 |  | $4 | $1 |  | $2 |  |  |
|  |  |  | $2 |  |  |  |  | $1 |
|  | $1 |  |  |  | $3 |  |  |  |

| | | | | | | | | |
|---|---|---|---|---|---|---|---|---|
|  |  | $1 |  |  | $3 |  | $2 |  |
| $3 | $4 |  |  |  |  | $1 |  |  |
| $1 |  |  |  | $2 |  |  | $4 |  |

| | | | | | | | | |
|---|---|---|---|---|---|---|---|---|
|  | $2 |  |  |  | $2 |  | $3 |  |
| $1 |  |  |  | $1 |  |  |  |  |
|  |  | $4 | $2 |  | $3 |  |  | $1 |

# Money Bingo £100

**Start:**                                    **End:**

|  |  |  |  |  |  |  |  |  |
|---|---|---|---|---|---|---|---|---|
| $5 |  | $3 |  | $1 |  |  | $1 |  |
|  |  | $1 | $4 |  |  |  |  | $2 |
|  | $2 |  |  | $2 | $3 |  |  |  |

|  |  |  |  |  |  |  |  |  |
|---|---|---|---|---|---|---|---|---|
|  |  |  | $3 | $1 |  |  |  | $4 |
| $2 |  | $3 |  |  |  |  | $1 |  |
|  |  |  | $1 |  |  | $1 | $2 |  |

|  |  |  |  |  |  |  |  |  |
|---|---|---|---|---|---|---|---|---|
|  | $3 |  | $3 | $1 |  | $2 |  |  |
|  |  |  | $2 |  |  |  |  | $1 |
|  | $1 |  |  |  | $3 |  |  |  |

|  |  |  |  |  |  |  |  |  |
|---|---|---|---|---|---|---|---|---|
|  |  | $1 |  |  | $3 |  | $2 |  |
| $3 | $4 |  |  |  |  | $1 |  |  |
|  |  |  |  | $2 |  |  | $5 |  |

|  |  |  |  |  |  |  |  |  |
|---|---|---|---|---|---|---|---|---|
|  | $2 |  |  |  | $2 |  | $3 |  |
| $1 |  |  |  | $1 |  |  |  | $1 |
|  |  | $4 | $3 |  | $3 |  |  | $1 |

# Money Bingo £100

Start:           End:

| | | | | | | | | |
|---|---|---|---|---|---|---|---|---|
| | $1 | | $2 | $1 | | | $1 | |
| | | | | | $2 | $3 | | |
| $5 | $3 | | | | | | | $2 |

| | | | | | | | | |
|---|---|---|---|---|---|---|---|---|
| $1 | | | $3 | $1 | $5 | | | |
| | | | | | | $1 | $1 | |
| | $4 | $2 | | | | | | $2 |

| | | | | | | | | |
|---|---|---|---|---|---|---|---|---|
| | | $1 | | $1 | | $2 | | |
| $4 | | | $2 | | | | | |
| | $3 | | | | $1 | | $3 | |

| | | | | | | | | |
|---|---|---|---|---|---|---|---|---|
| $4 | | $1 | $1 | | | | $2 | |
| | $1 | | | | | | | $5 |
| | | | $3 | $2 | | $3 | | |

| | | | | | | | | |
|---|---|---|---|---|---|---|---|---|
| | $2 | | $3 | | $2 | | | $3 |
| | | $1 | | $1 | | $1 | | |
| $4 | | | | | $3 | | | $1 |

 # Money Bingo £100 

**Start:**                    **End:**

|   |   |   |   |   |   |   |   |   |
|---|---|---|---|---|---|---|---|---|
|   |   | $3 | $1 |   |   |   | $1 |   |
| $3 |   |   |   |   | $1 |   |   |   |
|   | $2 |   | $5 | $2 |   |   |   | $2 |

|   |   |   |   |   |   |   |   |   |
|---|---|---|---|---|---|---|---|---|
| $2 |   |   | $3 | $1 |   | $5 |   |   |
|   |   | $1 |   |   |   |   | $1 | $2 |
|   |   |   |   | $4 |   | $1 |   |   |

|   |   |   |   |   |   |   |   |   |
|---|---|---|---|---|---|---|---|---|
|   |   |   |   | $2 |   | $1 |   |   |
| $3 | $1 |   |   |   |   |   |   | $3 |
|   |   | $4 | $1 |   |   |   | $2 |   |

|   |   |   |   |   |   |   |   |   |
|---|---|---|---|---|---|---|---|---|
| $3 |   | $1 |   |   | $3 | $5 |   |   |
|   |   |   | $2 |   |   |   |   |   |
| $1 |   |   |   | $4 |   |   | $1 | $2 |

|   |   |   |   |   |   |   |   |   |
|---|---|---|---|---|---|---|---|---|
|   | $2 | $3 |   |   | $2 |   |   |   |
| $1 |   |   |   | $1 |   |   | $4 |   |
|   | $3 |   | $3 |   |   | $1 |   | $1 |

#  Money Bingo £250 

Start:                    End:

| | | | | | | | | | |
|---|---|---|---|---|---|---|---|---|---|
| $5 | | $5 | | $7 | | | $6 | | |
| | | $4 | $5 | | | | | | $7 |
| | $8 | | | $5 | $3 | | | | |

| | | | | | | | | | |
|---|---|---|---|---|---|---|---|---|---|
| | | | $3 | $8 | | | | | $10 |
| $7 | | $6 | | | | | | $3 | |
| | | | $4 | | | | $5 | $7 | |

| | | | | | | | | | |
|---|---|---|---|---|---|---|---|---|---|
| | $10 | | $4 | | $5 | | $4 | | |
| | | | $7 | | | | | | $5 |
| | $3 | | | | | $3 | | | |

| | | | | | | | | | |
|---|---|---|---|---|---|---|---|---|---|
| | | $5 | | | | $6 | | $2 | |
| $8 | $4 | | | | | | $5 | | |
| $2 | | | | | $7 | | | $7 | |

| | | | | | | | | | |
|---|---|---|---|---|---|---|---|---|---|
| | $3 | | | | | $6 | | $8 | |
| $7 | | | | $10 | | | | | $2 |
| | | $4 | $6 | | $5 | | | | $4 |

 # Money Bingo £250 

Start:                                                        End:

| | | | | | | | | |
|---|---|---|---|---|---|---|---|---|
| | $10 | $6 | | | $3 | | $8 | |
| $3 | | | | $7 | | $5 | | |
| | | $5 | $4 | | | | | $4 |

| | | | | | | | | |
|---|---|---|---|---|---|---|---|---|
| | | | $4 | | $6 | | $6 | |
| | $8 | | | $6 | | $4 | | |
| $6 | | | | $5 | | | | $8 |

| | | | | | | | | |
|---|---|---|---|---|---|---|---|---|
| $10 | | | $6 | | | $4 | | $4 |
| | | | | $5 | | | | |
| | $5 | $4 | | | | | $3 | |

| | | | | | | | | |
|---|---|---|---|---|---|---|---|---|
| | | $8 | $7 | | | | | |
| | | | | $4 | | $4 | | $6 |
| $3 | $5 | | | | | $9 | | |

| | | | | | | | | |
|---|---|---|---|---|---|---|---|---|
| $9 | $3 | | $3 | | $6 | | | |
| | | $4 | | | | $2 | $11 | |
| | | | $8 | | | | $6 | $3 |

# Money Bingo £250

Start:                                    End:

| | | | | | | | | |
|---|---|---|---|---|---|---|---|---|
| | | $5 | $8 | $7 | | | | $6 |
| $3 | | | $6 | | | $4 | | |
| $4 | | | | $5 | | | $7 | |

| | | | | | | | | |
|---|---|---|---|---|---|---|---|---|
| | $5 | | | $9 | | | | $3 |
| | | $6 | | | | | | |
| $7 | | | $4 | | $3 | | $7 | $9 |

| | | | | | | | | |
|---|---|---|---|---|---|---|---|---|
| $9 | | $5 | | | | | | |
| | $3 | | | $4 | | | $4 | |
| | | | $8 | | $3 | $5 | | |

| | | | | | | | | |
|---|---|---|---|---|---|---|---|---|
| $7 | | $4 | | | | | $2 | |
| | $4 | | | $2 | $6 | | | $8 |
| | | | $6 | | | | $7 | |

| | | | | | | | | |
|---|---|---|---|---|---|---|---|---|
| $7 | | | $3 | | $5 | | $4 | |
| | $6 | | | $10 | | | | $3 |
| $4 | | | | | $5 | $8 | | |

# Money Bingo £250

Start:       End:

| | | | | | | | | |
|---|---|---|---|---|---|---|---|---|
| $4 | | | $6 | | | | $7 | $4 |
| | | $5 | | | $6 | | | |
| $4 | $2 | | | $8 | | | | $9 |

| | | | | | | | | |
|---|---|---|---|---|---|---|---|---|
| | $4 | | | $9 | | | | $4 |
| | | $7 | | | | | | |
| $9 | | | $4 | | $5 | | $6 | $7 |

| | | | | | | | | |
|---|---|---|---|---|---|---|---|---|
| $7 | | $5 | | | | | | |
| | $4 | | | $3 | | | $3 | |
| | | | $9 | | $6 | $4 | | |

| | | | | | | | | |
|---|---|---|---|---|---|---|---|---|
| $7 | | $4 | | | | | $2 | |
| | $3 | | | $3 | $6 | | | $8 |
| | | | $7 | | | | $6 | |

| | | | | | | | | |
|---|---|---|---|---|---|---|---|---|
| $6 | | | $4 | | $4 | | $5 | |
| | $7 | | | $9 | | | | $3 |
| $3 | | | | | $5 | $9 | | |

# Money Bingo £500

**Start:**                    **End:**

|  |  |  |  |  |  |  |  |  |
| --- | --- | --- | --- | --- | --- | --- | --- | --- |
| $9 |  | $11 |  | $9 |  |  | $15 |  |
|  |  | $7 | $10 |  |  |  |  | $9 |
|  | $8 |  |  | $15 | $7 |  |  |  |

|  |  |  |  |  |  |  |  |  |
| --- | --- | --- | --- | --- | --- | --- | --- | --- |
|  |  |  | $12 | $10 |  |  |  | $9 |
| $14 |  | $8 |  |  |  |  | $12 |  |
|  |  |  | $9 |  |  | $10 | $7 |  |

|  |  |  |  |  |  |  |  |  |
| --- | --- | --- | --- | --- | --- | --- | --- | --- |
|  | $10 |  | $9 | $14 |  | $17 |  |  |
|  |  |  | $11 |  |  |  |  | $13 |
|  | $15 |  |  |  | $8 |  |  |  |

|  |  |  |  |  |  |  |  |  |
| --- | --- | --- | --- | --- | --- | --- | --- | --- |
|  |  | $15 |  |  | $16 |  | $20 |  |
| $14 | $9 |  |  |  |  | $9 |  |  |
| $12 |  |  |  | $12 |  |  | $17 |  |

|  |  |  |  |  |  |  |  |  |
| --- | --- | --- | --- | --- | --- | --- | --- | --- |
|  | $9 |  |  |  | $8 |  | $10 |  |
| $10 |  |  |  | $10 |  |  |  | $11 |
|  |  | $8 | $15 |  | $7 |  |  |  |

 # Money Bingo £500 

Start:                                        End:

| | | | | | | | | |
|---|---|---|---|---|---|---|---|---|
| | | | | $10 | | $9 | | |
| | $8 | $7 | | | | | $15 | |
| $8 | | | $13 | $14 | $7 | | | $9 |

| | | | | | | | | |
|---|---|---|---|---|---|---|---|---|
| | $13 | | $12 | | | | | |
| | | $8 | | | $10 | | $8 | $9 |
| $12 | | | | $9 | | $10 | | |

| | | | | | | | | |
|---|---|---|---|---|---|---|---|---|
| $11 | | | | $14 | | | $18 | |
| | $8 | | | | $12 | | | |
| | | | $11 | | $11 | | | $12 |

| | | | | | | | | |
|---|---|---|---|---|---|---|---|---|
| | $9 | $14 | | | $17 | | $19 | $17 |
| | | | | | | | $10 | |
| $16 | | $12 | | $10 | | | | |

| | | | | | | | | |
|---|---|---|---|---|---|---|---|---|
| | | $8 | | | $9 | | $10 | $9 |
| $8 | | | $17 | $12 | | | | |
| | $9 | | | | | $6 | | |

# Money Bingo £500

Start:        End:

| | | | | | | | | | |
|---|---|---|---|---|---|---|---|---|---|
| | | | $9 | $10 | | $10 | | | |
| $10 | $6 | | | | $7 | | | | $11 |
| | $12 | | $13 | | | $12 | | | |

| | | | | | | | | | |
|---|---|---|---|---|---|---|---|---|---|
| $13 | | | | | $7 | | $7 | | |
| | $17 | $11 | | | | $10 | | | |
| | | | $9 | $15 | | | | | $11 |

| | | | | | | | | | |
|---|---|---|---|---|---|---|---|---|---|
| | $9 | | | | $10 | | | $16 | |
| $12 | | | | $11 | | $17 | | | |
| | | $10 | | $15 | | | | | |

| | | | | | | | | | |
|---|---|---|---|---|---|---|---|---|---|
| | | | $11 | | | | | | |
| | $10 | | | $7 | | | | $14 | |
| $16 | $17 | | | | | $10 | $15 | | |

| | | | | | | | | | |
|---|---|---|---|---|---|---|---|---|---|
| $11 | | | $8 | | | | | | |
| | $9 | | | | | $10 | $15 | | $12 |
| | | $14 | | $12 | | | | $9 | |

 # Money Bingo £500 

**Start:**                    **End:**

| | | | | | | | | |
|---|---|---|---|---|---|---|---|---|
| | | | $9 | | $8 | | | $7 |
| $10 | | $16 | | | | $10 | $12 | |
| | $6 | | | $13 | $9 | | | |

| | | | | | | | | |
|---|---|---|---|---|---|---|---|---|
| | | $17 | | | | | $8 | |
| $14 | | | | $11 | $10 | | | |
| $10 | | | $8 | | | $12 | | $10 |

| | | | | | | | | |
|---|---|---|---|---|---|---|---|---|
| $15 | | | $10 | | | | | $10 |
| | | | $14 | | $16 | | | $18 |
| | $9 | | | | | $8 | | |

| | | | | | | | | |
|---|---|---|---|---|---|---|---|---|
| | $8 | | | $10 | | $9 | | |
| $19 | | | $12 | | | | | |
| | $10 | | | | $15 | | $17 | |

| | | | | | | | | |
|---|---|---|---|---|---|---|---|---|
| $12 | | | $10 | | $13 | | | |
| | | $16 | | | | $9 | $14 | |
| $8 | | | | $11 | | | | $7 |

# Money Bingo £1000

Start:                                        End:

| | | | | | | | | |
|---|---|---|---|---|---|---|---|---|
| | | $18 | | | $9 | | | |
| $36 | | | $12 | $30 | | | | $10 |
| | $25 | $21 | | | $17 | | $22 | |

| | | | | | | | | |
|---|---|---|---|---|---|---|---|---|
| $22 | | | $23 | | | $18 | | $20 |
| | $26 | | | $25 | | | | |
| | | | $18 | $27 | | | $21 | |

| | | | | | | | | |
|---|---|---|---|---|---|---|---|---|
| | | $16 | | | | | $35 | |
| | $25 | | | $32 | | $28 | | |
| $23 | | | $19 | | | | | $22 |

| | | | | | | | | |
|---|---|---|---|---|---|---|---|---|
| | | $25 | | | $29 | | $26 | |
| $22 | $18 | | | | | $21 | | |
| $30 | | | | $19 | | | $10 | |

| | | | | | | | | |
|---|---|---|---|---|---|---|---|---|
| $26 | $23 | | $30 | | | | | $11 |
| | | $17 | | | $24 | | | |
| | | | | $20 | | $18 | $31 | |

#  Money Bingo £1000

Start:            End:

|  |  |  |  |  |  |  |  |  |
|---|---|---|---|---|---|---|---|---|
|  |  | $18 |  | $24 | $26 |  |  |  |
| $33 | $21 |  |  |  |  |  | $12 |  |
|  |  |  | $27 | $19 |  | $20 |  |  |

|  |  |  |  |  |  |  |  |  |
|---|---|---|---|---|---|---|---|---|
| $25 | $28 |  |  |  | $21 |  |  |  |
|  |  |  | $32 |  |  | $17 |  |  |
|  |  | $21 |  |  | $29 |  |  | $27 |

|  |  |  |  |  |  |  |  |  |
|---|---|---|---|---|---|---|---|---|
|  | $20 |  |  | $21 |  |  | $27 |  |
|  | $24 |  |  |  |  | $25 |  | $24 |
| $26 |  |  |  |  | $33 |  |  |  |

|  |  |  |  |  |  |  |  |  |
|---|---|---|---|---|---|---|---|---|
|  |  |  | $26 | $18 |  |  |  |  |
| $19 | $30 |  |  |  | $29 |  | $16 |  |
|  |  | $22 |  |  | $23 |  |  | $17 |

|  |  |  |  |  |  |  |  |  |
|---|---|---|---|---|---|---|---|---|
| $28 |  |  |  | $31 |  | $21 |  |  |
|  |  |  | $28 |  |  |  | $32 | $17 |
|  | $19 | $24 |  |  | $20 |  |  |  |

# Money Bingo £2000

Start:                              End:

| | | | | | | | | |
|---|---|---|---|---|---|---|---|---|
| $35 | | $39 | | $33 | | | $30 | |
| | | $36 | $50 | | | | | $41 |
| | $43 | | | $45 | $32 | | | |

| | | | | | | | | |
|---|---|---|---|---|---|---|---|---|
| | | | $46 | $50 | | | | $32 |
| $45 | | $41 | | | | | $37 | |
| | | | $33 | | | $48 | $55 | |

| | | | | | | | | |
|---|---|---|---|---|---|---|---|---|
| | $60 | | $35 | $50 | | $62 | | |
| | | | $56 | | | | | $52 |
| | $39 | | | | $48 | | | |

| | | | | | | | | |
|---|---|---|---|---|---|---|---|---|
| | | $47 | | | $57 | | $60 | |
| $60 | $55 | | | | | $52 | | |
| $38 | | | | $62 | | | $48 | |

| | | | | | | | | |
|---|---|---|---|---|---|---|---|---|
| | $39 | | | | $35 | | $25 | |
| $45 | | | | $50 | | | | $14 |
| | | $52 | $48 | | $40 | | | |

Start:                               End:

| | | | | | | | | |
|---|---|---|---|---|---|---|---|---|
| | | $33 | | $39 | $32 | | | $45 |
| | $50 | | $31 | | | $30 | | |
| $43 | | | | | | $36 | $45 | |

| | | | | | | | | |
|---|---|---|---|---|---|---|---|---|
| $41 | | | | | | $55 | | |
| $32 | | $33 | | | $45 | | | |
| | $46 | | $50 | $37 | | | | $48 |

| | | | | | | | | |
|---|---|---|---|---|---|---|---|---|
| | $62 | | | | $39 | $52 | | |
| | | $35 | $56 | | | | | |
| $48 | | | | | | | $50 | $60 |

| | | | | | | | | |
|---|---|---|---|---|---|---|---|---|
| $48 | | $60 | | $38 | | | | |
| | $62 | | | | | | | $57 |
| $47 | | | | $52 | $60 | | $55 | |

| | | | | | | | | |
|---|---|---|---|---|---|---|---|---|
| | $35 | $50 | $47 | | | $38 | | $35 |
| | | | $45 | | | | | |
| | $23 | | | | $48 | | | $27 |

#  Money Bingo £5000 

Start:                                    End:

| $100 |      | $113 |      | $102 |      |      | $100 |      |
|------|------|------|------|------|------|------|------|------|
|      |      | $133 | $95  |      |      |      |      | $105 |
|      | $120 |      |      | $116 | $90  |      |      |      |

| | | | $105 | $120 | | | | $102 |
|---|---|---|---|---|---|---|---|---|
| $97 | | $128 | | | | | | |
| | | | $111 | | | $135 | $95 | |

| | $140 | | $100 | $115 | | $150 | | |
|---|---|---|---|---|---|---|---|---|
| | | | $104 | | | | | $100 |
| | $128 | | | | $98 | | | |

| | | $100 | | | $147 | | $140 | |
|---|---|---|---|---|---|---|---|---|
| $140 | $135 | | | | | $141 | | |
| $138 | | | | $110 | | | $142 | |

| | $90 | | | | $138 | | $100 | |
|---|---|---|---|---|---|---|---|---|
| $100 | | | | $100 | | | | $67 |
| | | $107 | $123 | | $80 | | | |

# Money Bingo £5000

Start:                    End:

| | | | | | | | |
|---|---|---|---|---|---|---|---|
| | $118 | | $134 | | | $78 | $120 |
| | | | | | $103 | | |
| $123 | $95 | | | $100 | | $129 | |

| | | | | | | | |
|---|---|---|---|---|---|---|---|
| $100 | | | | $131 | $101 | | |
| $115 | | $127 | | | | $80 | $118 |
| | $95 | | | | | | $133 |

| | | | | | | | |
|---|---|---|---|---|---|---|---|
| $140 | | | $127 | $125 | | | |
| | | $90 | | | | | $145 |
| | $100 | | | $138 | $135 | | |

| | | | | | | | |
|---|---|---|---|---|---|---|---|
| | $120 | | | | $138 | | $100 |
| $130 | | | $90 | | | $96 | |
| | | $122 | | $117 | | | $87 |

| | | | | | | | |
|---|---|---|---|---|---|---|---|
| | | $105 | | | | | $101 |
| | $124 | | $131 | | $125 | | |
| $110 | | | $104 | | $100 | $100 | |

# Dollars In Days

Here you will find 30, and 60-day challenges. We have specifically added these so you can choose which works for you and what you are saving for, with saving amounts ranging from $50 up to $2000. You will also find blank sheets at the end of the 30 and 60-day sections where you can customize the amount you would like to save.

 # $50 in 30 days 

| | | | | |
|---|---|---|---|---|
| $2 | $1 | $1 | $2 | $1 |
| $1 | $2 | $1 | $3 | $2 |
| $2 | $2 | $2 | $1 | $2 |
| $3 | $2 | $1 | $1 | $1 |
| $1 | $2 | $1 | $1 | $2 |
| $2 | $2 | $2 | $2 | $2 |

| | | | | |
|---|---|---|---|---|
| $2 | $1 | $2 | $1 | $2 |
| $2 | $3 | $1 | $2 | $1 |
| $1 | $2 | $1 | $2 | $2 |
| $3 | $1 | $1 | $2 | $1 |
| $1 | $2 | $2 | $2 | $1 |
| $2 | $1 | $2 | $3 | $1 |

| | | | | |
|---|---|---|---|---|
| $3 | $2 | $1 | $1 | $2 |
| $2 | $1 | $2 | $1 | $1 |
| $1 | $1 | $2 | $3 | $2 |
| $1 | $1 | $2 | $1 | $3 |
| $2 | $2 | $1 | $2 | $1 |
| $1 | $3 | $2 | $2 | $1 |

# $50 in 30 days

| | | | | |
|---|---|---|---|---|
| $1 | $3 | $1 | $1 | $2 |
| $1 | $2 | $3 | $1 | $1 |
| $2 | $2 | $1 | $3 | $1 |
| $1 | $3 | $1 | $1 | $2 |
| $1 | $2 | $3 | $1 | $1 |
| $2 | $2 | $1 | $3 | $1 |

# $50 in 30 days

| | | | | |
|---|---|---|---|---|
| $2 | $2 | $1 | $1 | $2 |
| $1 | $2 | $3 | $2 | $2 |
| $3 | $1 | $1 | $2 | $2 |
| $1 | $3 | $1 | $2 | $1 |
| $2 | $2 | $1 | $3 | $1 |
| $1 | $1 | $1 | $1 | $2 |

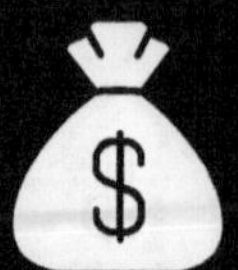

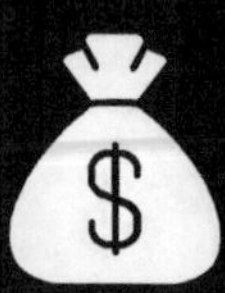

# $60 in 30 days

| | | | | |
|---|---|---|---|---|
| $2 | $2 | $2 | $2 | $2 |
| $2 | $2 | $2 | $2 | $2 |
| $2 | $2 | $2 | $2 | $2 |
| $2 | $2 | $2 | $2 | $2 |
| $2 | $2 | $2 | $2 | $2 |
| $2 | $2 | $2 | $2 | $2 |

# $60 in 30 days

| $2 | $2 | $2 | $2 | $2 |
|----|----|----|----|----|
| $2 | $2 | $2 | $2 | $2 |
| $2 | $2 | $2 | $2 | $2 |
| $2 | $2 | $2 | $2 | $2 |
| $2 | $2 | $2 | $2 | $2 |
| $2 | $2 | $2 | $2 | $2 |

 # $60 in 30 days 

| | | | | |
|---|---|---|---|---|
| $2 | $2 | $2 | $2 | $2 |
| $2 | $2 | $2 | $2 | $2 |
| $2 | $2 | $2 | $2 | $2 |
| $2 | $2 | $2 | $2 | $2 |
| $2 | $2 | $2 | $2 | $2 |
| $2 | $2 | $2 | $2 | $2 |

 # $60 in 30 days 

$2 $2 $2 $2 $2

$2 $2 $2 $2 $2

$2 $2 $2 $2 $2

$2 $2 $2 $2 $2

$2 $2 $2 $2 $2

$2 $2 $2 $2 $2

# $60 in 30 days

#  $100 in 30 days 

| | | | | |
|---|---|---|---|---|
| $5 | $3 | $4 | $3 | $3 |
| $2 | $2 | $5 | $2 | $4 |
| $2 | $5 | $3 | $4 | $3 |
| $3 | $4 | $2 | $2 | $5 |
| $3 | $2 | $5 | $3 | $4 |
| $2 | $3 | $4 | $5 | $3 |

$100 in 30 days



$4  $2  $4  $2  $4
$4  $6  $2  $4  $2
$2  $4  $2  $4  $4
$6  $2  $2  $4  $2
$2  $4  $4  $4  $2
$4  $2  $4  $6  $2

 # $100 in 30 days 

| | | | | |
|---|---|---|---|---|
| $2 | $3 | $4 | $5 | $2 |
| $3 | $2 | $3 | $5 | $4 |
| $4 | $3 | $4 | $5 | $3 |
| $2 | $4 | $4 | $3 | $2 |
| $3 | $2 | $2 | $4 | $3 |
| $5 | $5 | $3 | $4 | $2 |

# $100 in 30 days

| | | | | |
|---|---|---|---|---|
| $2 | $6 | $2 | $2 | $4 |
| $2 | $4 | $6 | $2 | $2 |
| $4 | $4 | $2 | $6 | $2 |
| $2 | $6 | $2 | $2 | $4 |
| $2 | $4 | $6 | $2 | $2 |
| $4 | $4 | $2 | $6 | $2 |

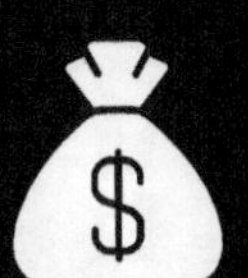

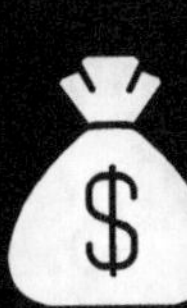

$100 in 30 days

$4
$3
$3
$2
$4
$3
$2
$3
$4
$3
$2
$3
$5
$4
$5
$5
$3
$3
$2
$4
$3
$2
$3
$4
$5
$4
$2
$5
$2
$3

 # $200 in 30 days 

| | | | | |
|---|---|---|---|---|
| $12 | $4 | $8 | $5 | $2 |
| $4 | $8 | $6 | $14 | $3 |
| $8 | $4 | $4 | $6 | $6 |
| $10 | $5 | $6 | $4 | $5 |
| $8 | $5 | $6 | $3 | $9 |
| $8 | $10 | $9 | $8 | $10 |

 # $200 in 30 days 

| | | | | |
|---|---|---|---|---|
| $8 | $12 | $5 | $9 | $7 |
| $6 | $9 | $14 | $10 | $8 |
| $3 | $10 | $5 | $7 | $5 |
| $4 | $9 | $7 | $4 | $3 |
| $6 | $3 | $5 | $2 | $10 |
| $7 | $3 | $8 | $3 | $8 |

$7 $6 $5 $7 $5

$9 $8 $8 $5 $7

$8 $7 $7 $8 $5

$5 $7 $8 $6 $7

$6 $8 $5 $6 $8

$5 $7 $5 $8 $7

$200 in 30 days



$5 $6 $7 $5 $9
$7 $6 $6 $8 $6
$9 $7 $6 $7 $5
$7 $6 $5 $8 $6
$8 $9 $6 $7 $5
$7 $8 $8 $6 $5

# $200 in 30 days

| | | | | |
|---|---|---|---|---|
| $7 | $8 | $7 | $6 | $6 |
| $7 | $5 | $6 | $5 | $9 |
| $8 | $6 | $6 | $7 | $7 |
| $5 | $8 | $7 | $8 | $6 |
| $6 | $8 | $6 | $7 | $5 |
| $7 | $8 | $5 | $6 | $8 |

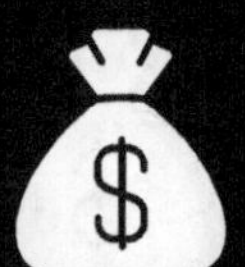

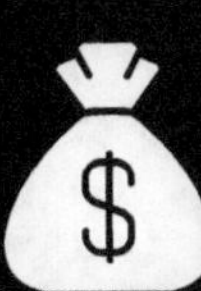

| | | | | |
|---|---|---|---|---|
| $12 | $12 | $12 | $12 | $12 |
| $12 | $12 | $12 | $12 | $12 |
| $12 | $12 | $12 | $12 | $12 |
| $12 | $12 | $12 | $12 | $12 |
| $12 | $12 | $12 | $12 | $12 |
| $12 | $12 | $12 | $12 | $12 |

#  $360 in 30 days 

| | | | | |
|---|---|---|---|---|
| $5 | $15 | $20 | $15 | $5 |
| $5 | $15 | $20 | $15 | $5 |
| $5 | $15 | $20 | $15 | $5 |
| $5 | $15 | $20 | $15 | $5 |
| $5 | $15 | $20 | $15 | $5 |
| $5 | $15 | $20 | $15 | $5 |

# $360 in 30 days

$12 $12 $12 $12 $12

$12 $12 $12 $12 $12

$12 $12 $12 $12 $12

$12 $12 $12 $12 $12

$12 $12 $12 $12 $12

$12 $12 $12 $12 $12

| | | | | |
|---|---|---|---|---|
| $10 | $15 | $10 | $15 | $10 |
| $10 | $15 | $10 | $15 | $10 |
| $10 | $15 | $10 | $15 | $10 |
| $10 | $15 | $10 | $15 | $10 |
| $10 | $15 | $10 | $15 | $10 |
| $10 | $15 | $10 | $15 | $10 |

# $360 in 30 days

| | | | | |
|---|---|---|---|---|
| $12 | $12 | $12 | $12 | $12 |
| $12 | $12 | $12 | $12 | $12 |
| $12 | $12 | $12 | $12 | $12 |
| $12 | $12 | $12 | $12 | $12 |
| $12 | $12 | $12 | $12 | $12 |
| $12 | $12 | $12 | $12 | $12 |

$
$450 in 30 days

$

$15 $15 $15 $15 $15
$15 $15 $15 $15 $15
$15 $15 $15 $15 $15
$15 $15 $15 $15 $15
$15 $15 $15 $15 $15
$15 $15 $15 $15 $15

 $450 in 30 days 

$10  $15  $25  $15  $10
$10  $15  $25  $15  $10
$10  $15  $25  $15  $10
$10  $15  $25  $15  $10
$10  $15  $25  $15  $10
$10  $15  $25  $15  $10

 # $450 in 30 days 

$15 $15 $15 $15 $15

$15 $15 $15 $15 $15

$15 $15 $15 $15 $15

$15 $15 $15 $15 $15

$15 $15 $15 $15 $15

$15 $15 $15 $15 $15

| | | | | |
|---|---|---|---|---|
| $5 | $10 | $15 | $20 | $25 |
| $5 | $10 | $15 | $20 | $25 |
| $5 | $10 | $15 | $20 | $25 |
| $5 | $10 | $15 | $20 | $25 |
| $5 | $10 | $15 | $20 | $25 |
| $5 | $10 | $15 | $20 | $25 |

$15 $15 $15 $15 $15
$15 $15 $15 $15 $15
$15 $15 $15 $15 $15
$15 $15 $15 $15 $15
$15 $15 $15 $15 $15
$15 $15 $15 $15 $15

$ in 30 days

$ ____ in 30 days

$ _____ in 30 days

$  in 30 days

|  |  |  |  |  |
|---|---|---|---|---|
| $5 | $4 | $3 | $2 | $1 |
| $5 | $4 | $3 | $2 | $1 |
| $5 | $4 | $3 | $2 | $1 |
| $5 | $4 | $3 | $2 | $1 |
| $5 | $4 | $3 | $2 | $1 |
| $5 | $4 | $3 | $2 | $1 |
| $5 | $4 | $3 | $2 | $1 |
| $5 | $4 | $3 | $2 | $1 |
| $5 | $4 | $3 | $2 | $1 |
| $5 | $4 | $3 | $2 | $1 |
| $5 | $4 | $3 | $2 | $1 |
| $5 | $4 | $3 | $2 | $1 |

#  $360 in 60 days 

| | | | | |
|---|---|---|---|---|
| $6 | $6 | $6 | $6 | $6 |
| $6 | $6 | $6 | $6 | $6 |
| $6 | $6 | $6 | $6 | $6 |
| $6 | $6 | $6 | $6 | $6 |
| $6 | $6 | $6 | $6 | $6 |
| $6 | $6 | $6 | $6 | $6 |
| $6 | $6 | $6 | $6 | $6 |
| $6 | $6 | $6 | $6 | $6 |
| $6 | $6 | $6 | $6 | $6 |
| $6 | $6 | $6 | $6 | $6 |

# $480 in 60 days

| $10 | $9 | $8 | $7 | $6 |
|-----|-----|-----|-----|-----|
| $10 | $9 | $8 | $7 | $6 |
| $10 | $9 | $8 | $7 | $6 |
| $10 | $9 | $8 | $7 | $6 |
| $10 | $9 | $8 | $7 | $6 |
| $10 | $9 | $8 | $7 | $6 |
| $10 | $9 | $8 | $7 | $6 |
| $10 | $9 | $8 | $7 | $6 |
| $10 | $9 | $8 | $7 | $6 |
| $10 | $9 | $8 | $7 | $6 |
| $10 | $9 | $8 | $7 | $6 |
| $10 | $9 | $8 | $7 | $6 |

 # $480 in 60 days 

| | | | | |
|---|---|---|---|---|
| $8 | $8 | $8 | $8 | $8 |
| $8 | $8 | $8 | $8 | $8 |
| $8 | $8 | $8 | $8 | $8 |
| $8 | $8 | $8 | $8 | $8 |
| $8 | $8 | $8 | $8 | $8 |
| $8 | $8 | $8 | $8 | $8 |
| $8 | $8 | $8 | $8 | $8 |
| $8 | $8 | $8 | $8 | $8 |
| $8 | $8 | $8 | $8 | $8 |
| $8 | $8 | $8 | $8 | $8 |

# $550 in 60 days

| | | | | | |
|---|---|---|---|---|---|
| $15 | $10 | $5 | $10 | $5 | $10 |
| $5 | $15 | $5 | $10 | $5 | $15 |
| $5 | $10 | $15 | $10 | $5 | $10 |
| $5 | $10 | $5 | $10 | $15 | $10 |
| $15 | $10 | $5 | $10 | $5 | $10 |
| $5 | $15 | $5 | $10 | $5 | $15 |
| $5 | $10 | $15 | $10 | $5 | $10 |
| $5 | $10 | $5 | $10 | $15 | $10 |
| $15 | $10 | $5 | $10 | $5 | $10 |
| $5 | $15 | $5 | $10 | $5 | $15 |

# $600 in 60 days

## TODO

$10 $10 $10 $10 $10
$10 $10 $10 $10 $10
$10 $10 $10 $10 $10
$10 $10 $10 $10 $10
$10 $10 $10 $10 $10
$10 $10 $10 $10 $10
$10 $10 $10 $10 $10
$10 $10 $10 $10 $10
$10 $10 $10 $10 $10
$10 $10 $10 $10 $10
$10 $10 $10 $10 $10
$10 $10 $10 $10 $10

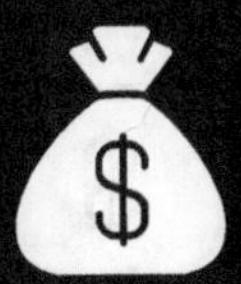

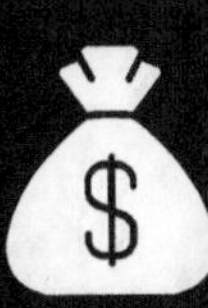

| | | | | | |
|---|---|---|---|---|---|
| $5 | $15 | $5 | $15 | $5 | $15 |
| $5 | $15 | $5 | $15 | $5 | $15 |
| $5 | $15 | $5 | $15 | $5 | $15 |
| $5 | $15 | $5 | $15 | $5 | $15 |
| $5 | $15 | $5 | $15 | $5 | $15 |
| $5 | $15 | $5 | $15 | $5 | $15 |
| $5 | $15 | $5 | $15 | $5 | $15 |
| $5 | $15 | $5 | $15 | $5 | $15 |
| $5 | $15 | $5 | $15 | $5 | $15 |
| $5 | $15 | $5 | $15 | $5 | $15 |

| $13 | $13 | $13 | $13 | $13 |
|---|---|---|---|---|
| $13 | $13 | $13 | $13 | $13 |
| $13 | $13 | $13 | $13 | $13 |
| $13 | $13 | $13 | $13 | $13 |
| $13 | $13 | $13 | $13 | $13 |
| $13 | $13 | $13 | $13 | $13 |
| $13 | $13 | $13 | $13 | $13 |
| $13 | $13 | $13 | $13 | $13 |
| $13 | $13 | $13 | $13 | $13 |
| $13 | $13 | $13 | $13 | $13 |
| $13 | $13 | $13 | $13 | $13 |
| $13 | $13 | $13 | $13 | $13 |

# $900 in 60 days

| | | | | | |
|---|---|---|---|---|---|
| $15 | $15 | $15 | $15 | $15 | $15 |
| $15 | $15 | $15 | $15 | $15 | $15 |
| $15 | $15 | $15 | $15 | $15 | $15 |
| $15 | $15 | $15 | $15 | $15 | $15 |
| $15 | $15 | $15 | $15 | $15 | $15 |
| $15 | $15 | $15 | $15 | $15 | $15 |
| $15 | $15 | $15 | $15 | $15 | $15 |
| $15 | $15 | $15 | $15 | $15 | $15 |
| $15 | $15 | $15 | $15 | $15 | $15 |
| $15 | $15 | $15 | $15 | $15 | $15 |

$20 $20 $10 $10 $20 $20
$10 $10 $20 $20 $20 $20
$20 $20 $20 $20 $10 $10
$20 $20 $10 $10 $20 $20
$10 $10 $20 $20 $20 $20
$20 $20 $20 $20 $10 $10
$20 $20 $10 $10 $20 $20
$10 $10 $20 $20 $20 $20
$20 $20 $20 $20 $10 $10
$20 $20 $10 $10 $20 $20

# $1000 in 60 days

# $1200 in 60 days

| | | | | | |
|---|---|---|---|---|---|
| $20 | $20 | $20 | $20 | $20 | $20 |
| $20 | $20 | $20 | $20 | $20 | $20 |
| $20 | $20 | $20 | $20 | $20 | $20 |
| $20 | $20 | $20 | $20 | $20 | $20 |
| $20 | $20 | $20 | $20 | $20 | $20 |
| $20 | $20 | $20 | $20 | $20 | $20 |
| $20 | $20 | $20 | $20 | $20 | $20 |
| $20 | $20 | $20 | $20 | $20 | $20 |
| $20 | $20 | $20 | $20 | $20 | $20 |
| $20 | $20 | $20 | $20 | $20 | $20 |

| $30 | $15 | $35 | $15 | $30 |
|---|---|---|---|---|
| $30 | $15 | $35 | $15 | $30 |
| $30 | $15 | $35 | $15 | $30 |
| $30 | $15 | $35 | $15 | $30 |
| $30 | $15 | $35 | $15 | $30 |
| $30 | $15 | $35 | $15 | $30 |
| $30 | $15 | $35 | $15 | $30 |
| $30 | $15 | $35 | $15 | $30 |
| $30 | $15 | $35 | $15 | $30 |
| $30 | $15 | $35 | $15 | $30 |
| $30 | $15 | $35 | $15 | $30 |
| $30 | $15 | $35 | $15 | $30 |

#  $1800 in 60 days 

| | | | | | |
|---|---|---|---|---|---|
| $30 | $30 | $30 | $30 | $30 | $30 |
| $30 | $30 | $30 | $30 | $30 | $30 |
| $30 | $30 | $30 | $30 | $30 | $30 |
| $30 | $30 | $30 | $30 | $30 | $30 |
| $30 | $30 | $30 | $30 | $30 | $30 |
| $30 | $30 | $30 | $30 | $30 | $30 |
| $30 | $30 | $30 | $30 | $30 | $30 |
| $30 | $30 | $30 | $30 | $30 | $30 |
| $30 | $30 | $30 | $30 | $30 | $30 |
| $30 | $30 | $30 | $30 | $30 | $30 |

$2000 in 60 days

$40 $25 $55 $35 $50 $45
$35 $55 $40 $50 $40 $40
$65 $25 $30 $45 $50 $35
$35 $55 $40 $60 $25 $35
$50 $50 $25 $30 $40 $55
$45 $35 $50 $55 $45 $20
$30 $50 $45 $35 $45 $45
$60 $25 $30 $55 $35 $45
$50 $40 $60 $45 $30 $25
$35 $50 $40 $45 $30 $50

 $  in 60 days 

$ in 60 days

$          in 60 days

# Timed challenge

In this section are savings challenges that are over 3, 6, 12, 18, and 24 month periods. These are ideal for all savings needs from short term to long term. Simply decide the amount you want to save and over which time period, then write the amount you will need to save each month. For example, if you choose to save $3,000 over 12 months you would divide 3,000 by 12 which is 250, so you would need to save $250 each month to achieve your goal. Top tip, write these amounts on the sheet in pencil, then you can rub them out and reuse the page!

# $ ___ in 3 months

How it works: Write the amount you would like to save above, then divide that number by 3, this is the number of dollars you need for each jar. You can choose to color in or just cross out the jars as you save the amounts.

Start date: ________   End date: ________   Amount per jar: ________

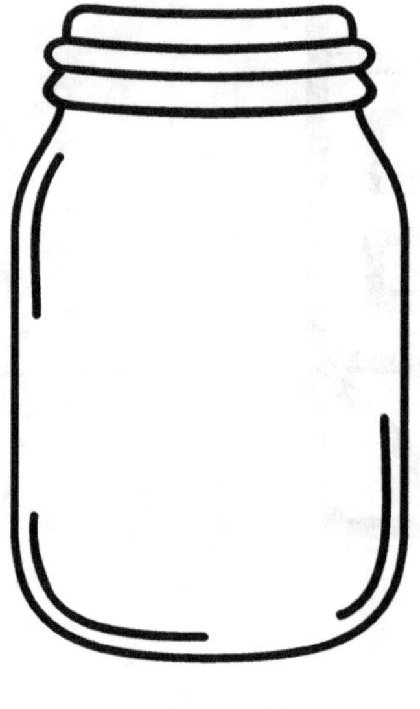 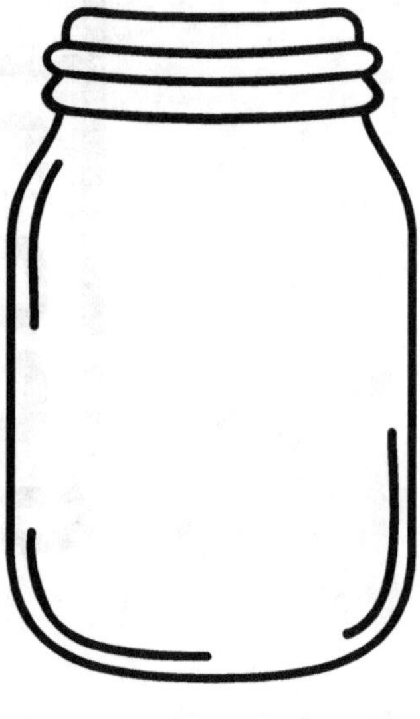

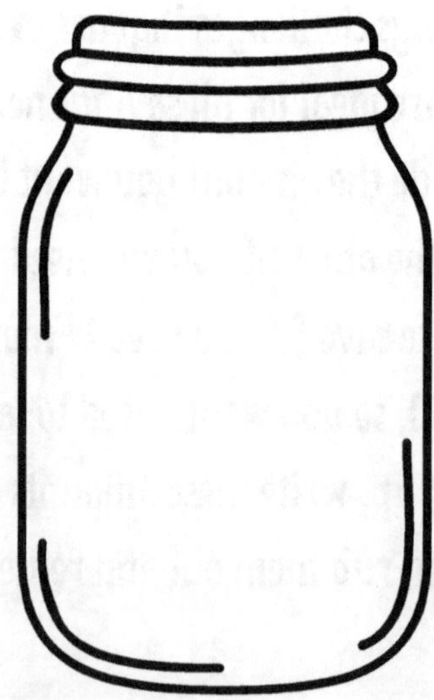

 # $ in 6 months 

How it works: Write the amount you would like to save above, then divide that number by 6, this is the number of dollars you need for each jar. You can choose to color in or just cross out the jars as you save the amounts.

**Start date:**          **End date:**          **Amount per jar:**

 # $ ___ in 9 months 

How it works: Write the amount you would like to save above, then divide that number by 9, this is the number of dollars you need for each jar. You can choose to color in or just cross out the jars as you save the amounts.

Start date: _______    End date: _______    Amount per jar: _______

 $ # in 12 months 

How it works: Write the amount you would like to save above, then divide that number by 12, this is the number of dollars you need for each jar. You can choose to color in or just cross out the jars as you save the amounts.

Start date:          End date:          Amount per jar:

 # $ ______ in 18 months 

**How it works:** Write the amount you would like to save above, then divide that number by 18, this is the number of dollars you need for each jar. You can choose to color in or just cross out the jars as you save the amounts.

Start date: ______     End date: ______     Amount per jar: ______

# $ in 24 months

**How it works: Write the amount you would like to save above, then divide that number by 24, this is the number of dollars you need for each jar. You can choose to color in or just cross out the jars as you save the amounts.**

**Start date:** **End date:** **Amount per jar:**

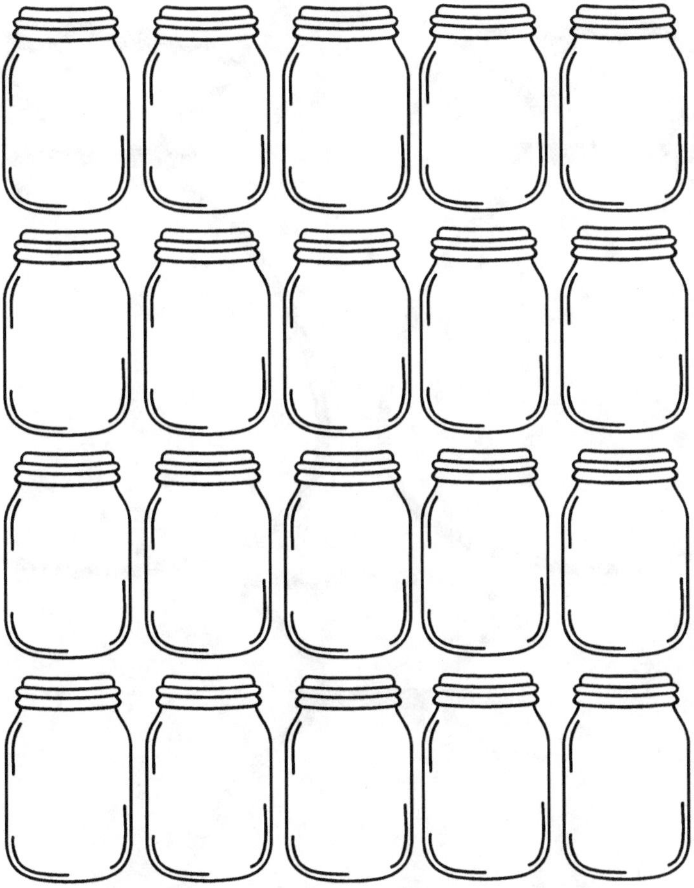

 # $ ____ in 3 months 

How it works: Write the amount you would like to save above, then divide that number by 3, this is the number of dollars you need for each jar. You can choose to color in or just cross out the bags as you save the amounts.

Start date: _______     End date: _______     Amount per jar: _______

 # $ _______ in 6 months 

---

How it works: Write the amount you would like to save above, then divide that number by 6, this is the number of dollars you need for each jar. You can choose to color in or just cross out the bags as you save the amounts.

Start date: _______     End date: _______     Amount per jar: _______

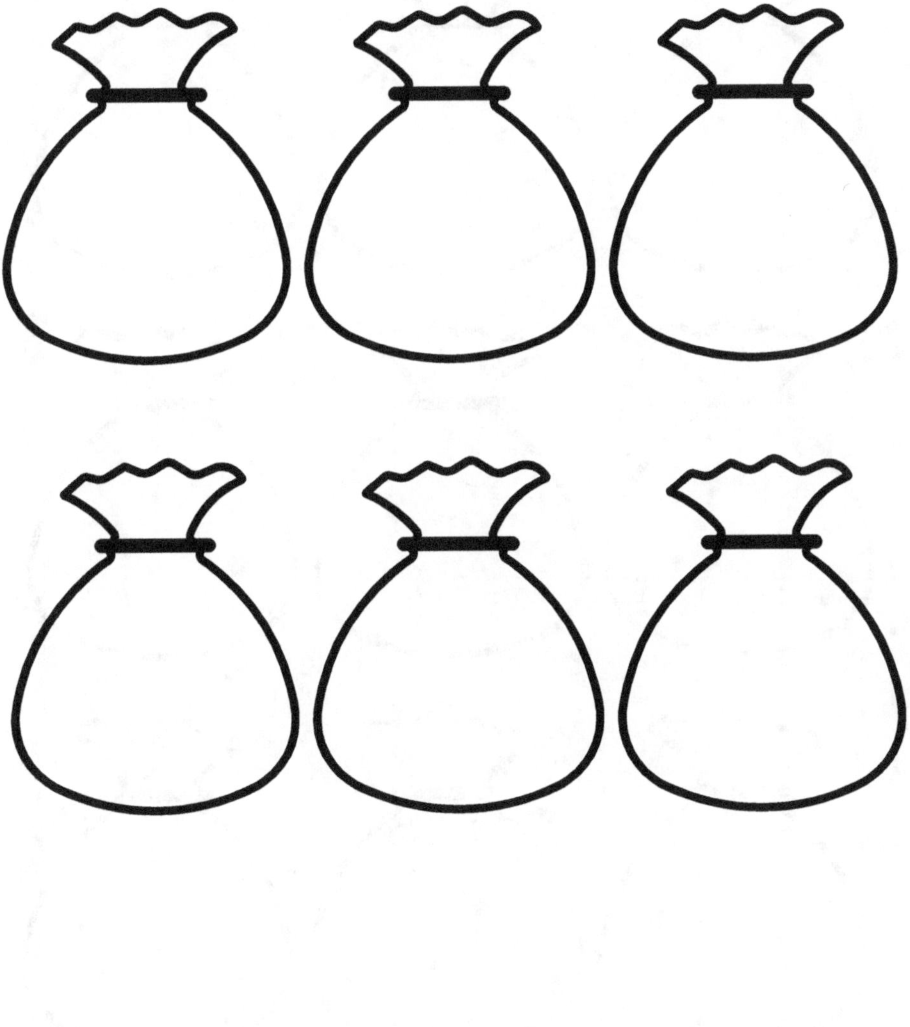

# $ ______ in 9 months

**How it works:** Write the amount you would like to save above, then divide that number by 9, this is the number of dollars you need for each jar. You can choose to color in or just cross out the bags as you save the amounts.

Start date: _______     End date: _______     Amount per jar: _______

 **$** # in 12 months 

How it works: Write the amount you would like to save above, then divide that number by 12, this is the number of dollars you need for each jar. You can choose to color in or just cross out the bags as you save the amounts.

**Start date:**          **End date:**          **Amount per jar:**

 # $ in 18 months 

**How it works:** Write the amount you would like to save above, then divide that number by 18, this is the number of dollars you need for each jar. You can choose to color in or just cross out the bags as you save the amounts.

Start date:        End date:        Amount per jar:

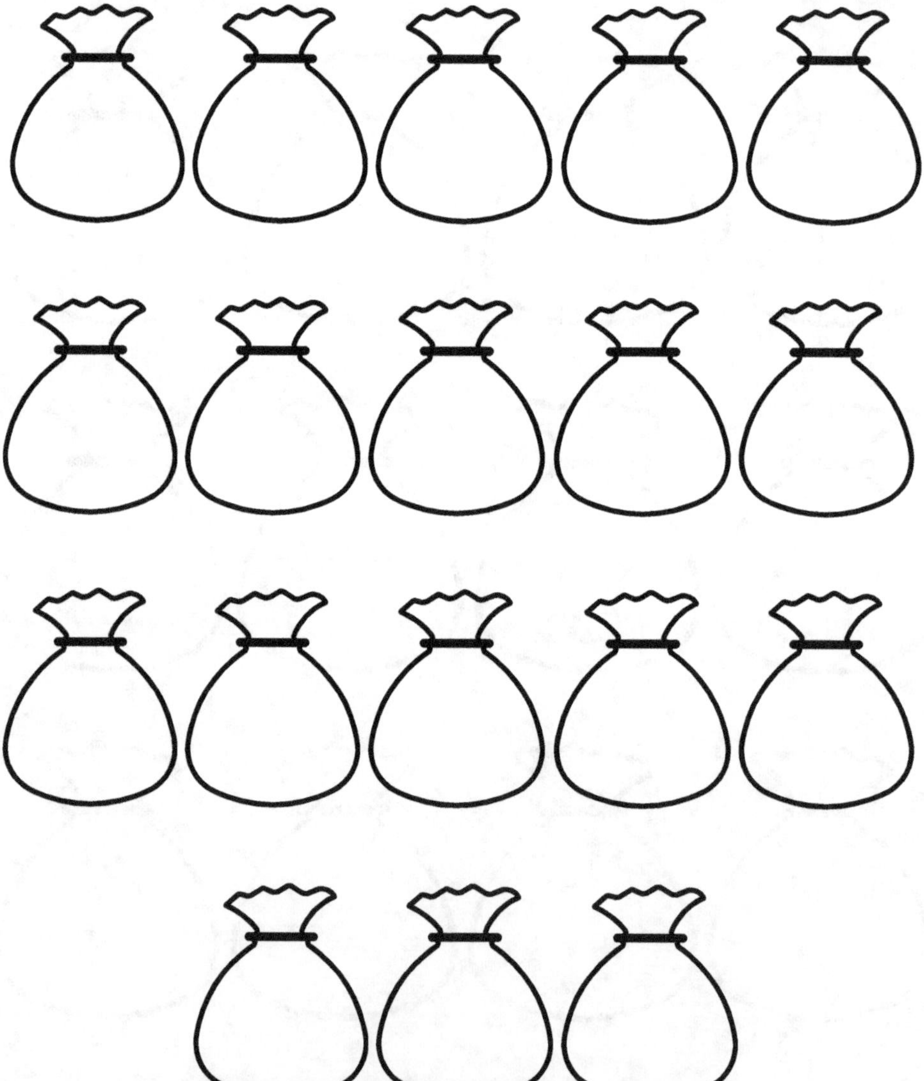

 $ # in 24 months 

**How it works:** Write the amount you would like to save above, then divide that number by 24, this is the number of dollars you need for each jar. You can choose to color in or just cross out the bags as you save the amounts.

**Start date:**        **End date:**        **Amount per jar:**

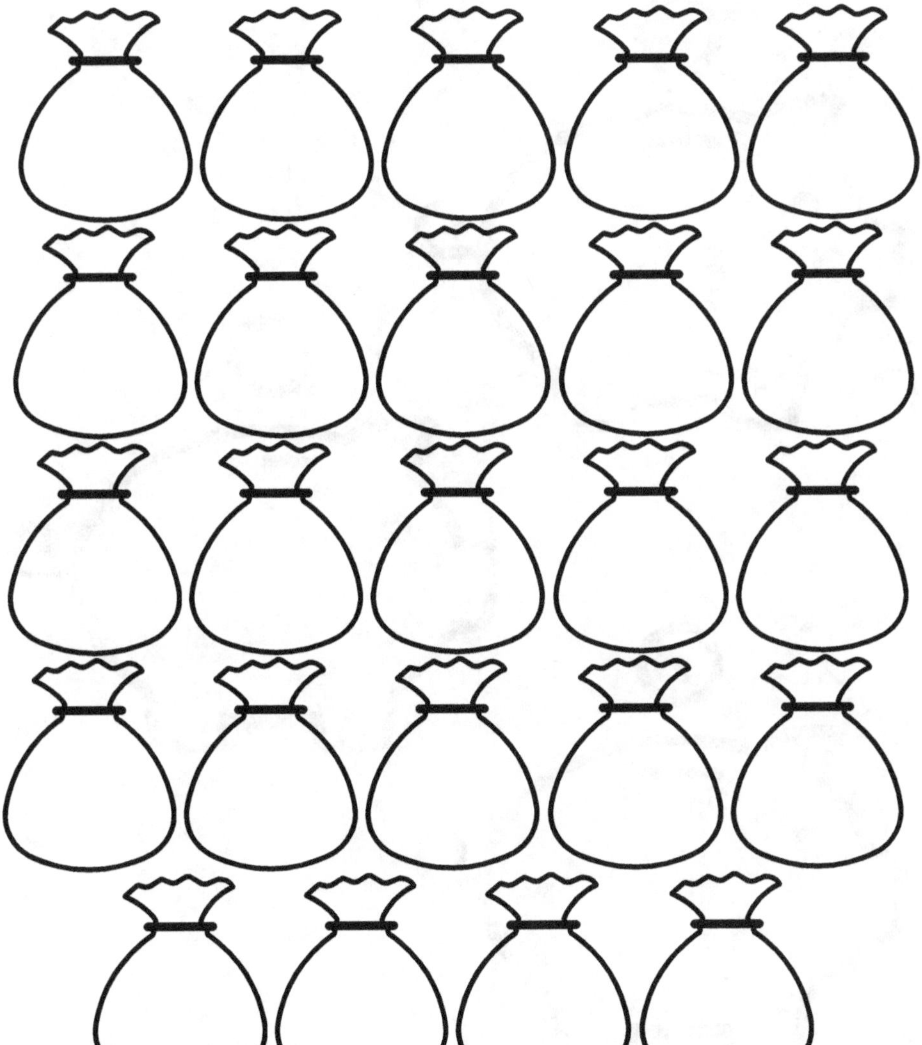

 # $ in 3 months 

**How it works:** Write the amount you would like to save above, then divide that number by 3, this is the number of dollars you need for each piggy bank. You can choose to color in or just cross out the bags as you save the amounts.

**Start date:**          **End date:**          **Amount per jar:**

# $ ______ in 6 months

How it works: Write the amount you would like to save above, then divide that number by 6, this is the number of dollars you need for each piggy bank. You can choose to color in or just cross out the bags as you save the amounts.

**Start date:** ______     **End date:** ______     **Amount per jar:** ______

# $ in 9 months

**How it works: Write the amount you would like to save above, then divide that number by 9, this is the number of dollars you need for each piggy bank. You can choose to color in or just cross out the bags as you save the amounts.**

**Start date:** **End date:** **Amount per jar:**

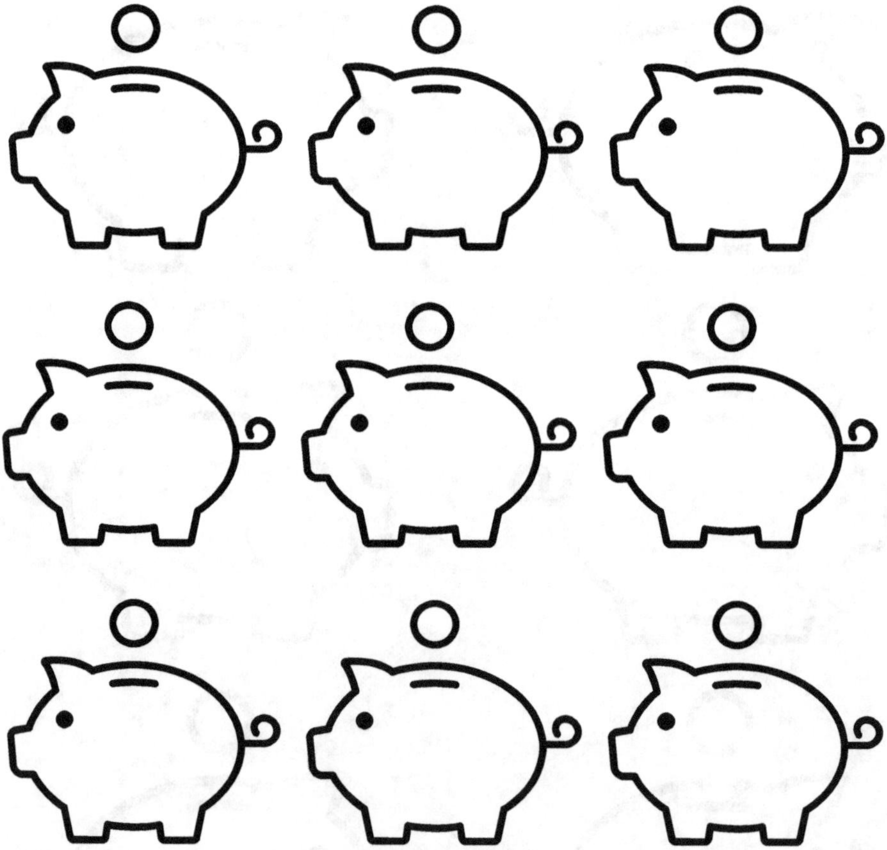

**How it works:** Write the amount you would like to save above, then divide that number by 12, this is the number of dollars you need for each piggy bank. You can choose to color in or just cross out the bags as you save the amounts.

Start date:      End date:      Amount per jar:

How it works: Write the amount you would like to save above, then divide that number by 18, this is the number of dollars you need for each piggy bank. You can choose to color in or just cross out the bags as you save the amounts.

Start date:        End date:        Amount per jar:

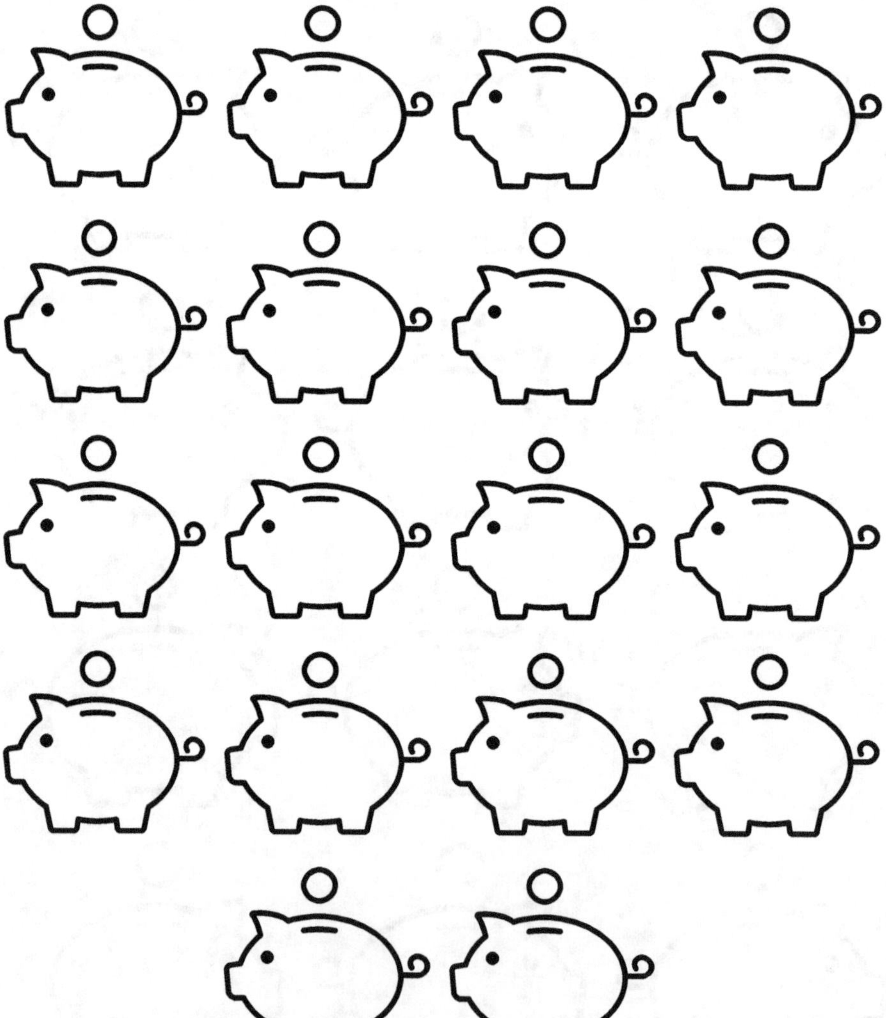

**How it works:** Write the amount you would like to save above, then divide that number by 24, this is the number of dollars you need for each piggy bank. You can choose to color in or just cross out the bags as you save the amounts.

| Start date: | End date: | Amount per jar: |
|---|---|---|

# Fund Pages

You will find 100 icons on each of the following pages, simply decide the amount you need to save, then divide it by 100 for the amount you need for each icon. For example, if you needed $20,000 you would simply take 20,000 and divide it by 100 = $200. So $200 is the amount you need to save, then you can cross off one of the house icons below. Every $200 you save you can cross off until all the icons have been crossed off and you have your $20,000!  We have also given you some blank pages at the end of the section for you to customize.

# Emergency Fund

**Goal amount**                    **Amount per icon:**

# House Fund

**Goal amount:**                    **Amount per icon:**

# College Fund

**Goal amount:** ________     **Amount per icon:** ________

# Wedding Fund

**Goal amount:**     **Amount per icon:**

 # Car Fund 

**Goal amount:**          **Amount per icon:**

# Baby Fund

**Goal amount:** **Amount per icon:**

# Christmas Fund

**Goal amount:**     **Amount per icon:**

# Vacation Fund

**Goal amount:** ______________          **Amount per icon:** ______________

# ___________Fund

**Goal amount:**     **Amount per icon:**

# _________ Fund

**Goal amount:**      **Amount per icon:**

_______________Fund

**Goal amount:**                    **Amount per icon:**

# _____________ Fund

**Goal amount:**          **Amount per icon:**

_____________Fund

**Goal amount:**         **Amount per icon:**

_______________ Fund

Goal amount:          Amount per icon:

# _____________ Fund

**Goal amount:** ___________     **Amount per icon:** ___________

_______________ Fund

**Goal amount:**                    **Amount per icon:**

# Roll the dice

Here you will find 31-day challenges, so no matter which month you choose to take the challenge, you will have one for every day. You will need a dice, then simply roll it and whatever number you get is the amount you need to save that day. Simply cross off the number on your dice and repeat each day for the month.

# Roll the dice

How it works: Roll the dice everyday and circle the number you got, the number of dots equals the number of dollars you need to save that day!

Month _______________     Amount saved _______________

Day 1     Day 2     Day 3     Day 4     Day 5     Day 6     Day 7     Day 8

Day 9     Day 10     Day 11     Day 12     Day 13     Day 14     Day 15     Day 16

Day 17     Day 18     Day 19     Day 20     Day 21     Day 22     Day 23     Day 24

Day 25     Day 26     Day 27     Day 28     Day 29     Day 30     Day 31

$

# Roll the dice

**How it works:** Roll the dice everyday and circle the number you got, the number of dots equals the number of dollars you need to save that day!

Month _______________     Amount saved _______________

Day 1  Day 2  Day 3  Day 4  Day 5  Day 6  Day 7  Day 8

Day 9  Day 10  Day 11  Day 12  Day 13  Day 14  Day 15  Day 16

Day 17  Day 18  Day 19  Day 20  Day 21  Day 22  Day 23  Day 24

Day 25  Day 26  Day 27  Day 28  Day 29  Day 30  Day 31

# Roll the dice

How it works: Roll the dice everyday and circle the number you got, the number of dots equals the number of dollars you need to save that day!

**Month** _______________          **Amount saved** _______________

Day 1    Day 2    Day 3    Day 4    Day 5    Day 6    Day 7    Day 8

Day 9    Day 10    Day 11    Day 12    Day 13    Day 14    Day 15    Day 16

Day 17    Day 18    Day 19    Day 20    Day 21    Day 22    Day 23    Day 24

Day 25    Day 26    Day 27    Day 28    Day 29    Day 30    Day 31

$

 # Roll the dice 

How it works: Roll the dice everyday and circle the number you got, the number of dots equals the number of dollars you need to save that day!

Month ________________          Amount saved ________________

| Day 1 | Day 2 | Day 3 | Day 4 | Day 5 | Day 6 | Day 7 | Day 8 |

| Day 9 | Day 10 | Day 11 | Day 12 | Day 13 | Day 14 | Day 15 | Day 16 |

| Day 17 | Day 18 | Day 19 | Day 20 | Day 21 | Day 22 | Day 23 | Day 24 |

| Day 25 | Day 26 | Day 27 | Day 28 | Day 29 | Day 30 | Day 31 | $ |

# Roll the dice



How it works: Roll the dice everyday and circle the number you got, the number o[f]
dots equals the number of dollars you need to save that day!

**Month** ______________          **Amount saved** ______________

Day 1    Day 2    Day 3    Day 4    Day 5    Day 6    Day 7    Day 8

Day 9    Day 10    Day 11    Day 12    Day 13    Day 14    Day 15    Day 16

Day 17    Day 18    Day 19    Day 20    Day 21    Day 22    Day 23    Day 24

Day 25    Day 26    Day 27    Day 28    Day 29    Day 30    Day 31

# Roll the dice

**How it works:** Roll the dice everyday and circle the number you got, the number of dots equals the number of dollars you need to save that day!

Month ________________     Amount saved ________________

Day 1  Day 2  Day 3  Day 4  Day 5  Day 6  Day 7  Day 8

Day 9  Day 10  Day 11  Day 12  Day 13  Day 14  Day 15  Day 16

Day 17  Day 18  Day 19  Day 20  Day 21  Day 22  Day 23  Day 24

Day 25  Day 26  Day 27  Day 28  Day 29  Day 30  Day 31

$

# Roll the dice

How it works: Roll the dice everyday and circle the number you got, the number of dots equals the number of dollars you need to save that day!

Month ________________    Amount saved ________________

Day 1    Day 2    Day 3    Day 4    Day 5    Day 6    Day 7    Day 8

Day 9    Day 10    Day 11    Day 12    Day 13    Day 14    Day 15    Day 16

Day 17    Day 18    Day 19    Day 20    Day 21    Day 22    Day 23    Day 24

Day 25    Day 26    Day 27    Day 28    Day 29    Day 30    Day 31

# Roll the dice

How it works: Roll the dice everyday and circle the number you got, the number of dots equals the number of dollars you need to save that day!

Month _______________     Amount saved _______________

Day 1  Day 2  Day 3  Day 4  Day 5  Day 6  Day 7  Day 8

Day 9  Day 10  Day 11  Day 12  Day 13  Day 14  Day 15  Day 16

Day 17  Day 18  Day 19  Day 20  Day 21  Day 22  Day 23  Day 24

Day 25  Day 26  Day 27  Day 28  Day 29  Day 30  Day 31

$

 # Roll the dice 

How it works: Roll the dice everyday and circle the number you got, the number of dots equals the number of dollars you need to save that day!

Month _______________          Amount saved _______________

Day 1   Day 2   Day 3   Day 4   Day 5   Day 6   Day 7   Day 8

Day 9   Day 10   Day 11   Day 12   Day 13   Day 14   Day 15   Day 16

Day 17   Day 18   Day 19   Day 20   Day 21   Day 22   Day 23   Day 24

Day 25   Day 26   Day 27   Day 28   Day 29   Day 30   Day 31

$

 # Roll the dice 

**How it works:** Roll the dice everyday and circle the number you got, the number of dots equals the number of dollars you need to save that day!

**Month** _______________     **Amount saved** _______________

Day 1     Day 2     Day 3     Day 4     Day 5     Day 6     Day 7     Day 8

Day 9     Day 10     Day 11     Day 12     Day 13     Day 14     Day 15     Day 16

Day 17     Day 18     Day 19     Day 20     Day 21     Day 22     Day 23     Day 24

Day 25     Day 26     Day 27     Day 28     Day 29     Day 30     Day 31

$

# Roll the dice

How it works: Roll the dice everyday and circle the number you got, the number o dots equals the number of dollars you need to save that day!

**Month** _______________          **Amount saved** _______________

Day 1     Day 2     Day 3     Day 4     Day 5     Day 6     Day 7     Day 8

Day 9     Day 10    Day 11    Day 12    Day 13    Day 14    Day 15    Day 16

Day 17    Day 18    Day 19    Day 20    Day 21    Day 22    Day 23    Day 24

Day 25    Day 26    Day 27    Day 28    Day 29    Day 30    Day 31

# Roll the dice

How it works: Roll the dice everyday and circle the number you got, the number of dots equals the number of dollars you need to save that day!

Month ________________          Amount saved ________________

Day 1  Day 2  Day 3  Day 4  Day 5  Day 6  Day 7  Day 8

Day 9  Day 10  Day 11  Day 12  Day 13  Day 14  Day 15  Day 16

Day 17  Day 18  Day 19  Day 20  Day 21  Day 22  Day 23  Day 24

Day 25  Day 26  Day 27  Day 28  Day 29  Day 30  Day 31

# Envelope Challenge

Here you will find 31-day challenges, so no matter which month you choose to take the challenge, you will have one for every day. The savings amounts vary from $31 up to $900. As always we have included blank sheets at the end of the section for you to customize your own amounts.

# $31 Envelope



**How it works:** Each day is $1, take your dollar and place it in a physical envelope then cross off or circle one envelope on this page until you cross or circle all the envelopes.

**Start date:**

$1  $1  $1  $1  $1

$1  $1  $1  $1  $1

$1  $1  $1  $1  $1

$1  $1  $1  $1  $1

$1  $1  $1  $1  $1

$1  $1  $1  $1  $1

$1

#  $62 Envelope 

**How it works:** Each day is $2, take your dollar and place it in a physical envelope then cross off or circle one envelope on this page until you cross or circle all the envelopes.

**Start date:**

| | | | | |
|---|---|---|---|---|
| $2 | $2 | $2 | $2 | $2 |
| $2 | $2 | $2 | $2 | $2 |
| $2 | $2 | $2 | $2 | $2 |
| $2 | $2 | $2 | $2 | $2 |
| $2 | $2 | $2 | $2 | $2 |
| $2 | $2 | $2 | $2 | $2 |
| $2 | | | | |

# $100 Envelope

How it works: Each day for 30 days pick an envelope, you can do them in order or not. Take the amount stated and place it in a physical envelope, and mark off on this sheet which envelope amount you saved.

Start date:

| | | | | |
|---|---|---|---|---|
| $5 | $1 | $3 | $6 | $5 |
| $1 | $7 | $6 | $5 | $3 |
| $4 | $2 | $2 | $6 | $3 |
| $4 | $1 | $3 | $5 | $2 |
| $1 | $7 | $2 | $4 | $1 |
| $1 | $2 | $1 | $2 | $5 |

# $150 Envelope

How it works: Each day is $5, take your $5 dollars and place it in a physical envelope then cross off or circle one envelope on this page until you cross or circle all the envelopes.

Start date:

| | | | | |
|---|---|---|---|---|
| $5 | $5 | $5 | $5 | $5 |
| $5 | $5 | $5 | $5 | $5 |
| $5 | $5 | $5 | $5 | $5 |
| $5 | $5 | $5 | $5 | $5 |
| $5 | $5 | $5 | $5 | $5 |
| $5 | $5 | $5 | $5 | $5 |

# $300 Envelope

How it works: Each day for 30 days pick an envelope, you can do them in order or not. Take the amount stated and place it in a physical envelope, and mark off on this sheet which envelope amount you saved.

**Start date:**

| | | | | |
|---|---|---|---|---|
| $15 | $3 | $9 | $18 | $15 |
| $3 | $21 | $18 | $15 | $9 |
| $12 | $6 | $6 | $18 | $9 |
| $12 | $3 | $9 | $15 | $6 |
| $3 | $21 | $6 | $12 | $3 |
| $3 | $6 | $3 | $6 | $3 |
| $12 | | | | |

# $300 Envelope

**How it works: Each day is $10, take your $10 dollars and place it in a physical envelope then cross off or circle one envelope on this page until you cross or circle all the envelopes.**

**Start date:**

| | | | | |
|---|---|---|---|---|
| $10 | $10 | $10 | $10 | $10 |
| $10 | $10 | $10 | $10 | $10 |
| $10 | $10 | $10 | $10 | $10 |
| $10 | $10 | $10 | $10 | $10 |
| $10 | $10 | $10 | $10 | $10 |
| $10 | $10 | $10 | $10 | $10 |

# $450 Envelope



**How it works:** Each day is $15, take your $15 dollars and place it in a physical envelope then cross off or circle one envelope on this page until you cross or circle all the envelopes.

**Start date:**

| | | | | |
|---|---|---|---|---|
| $15 | $15 | $15 | $15 | $15 |
| $15 | $15 | $15 | $15 | $15 |
| $15 | $15 | $15 | $15 | $15 |
| $15 | $15 | $15 | $15 | $15 |
| $15 | $15 | $15 | $15 | $15 |
| $15 | $15 | $15 | $15 | $15 |

#  $600 Envelope 

**How it works:** Each day is $20, take your $20 dollars and place it in a physical envelope then cross off or circle one envelope on this page until you cross or circle all the envelopes.

**Start date:**

| | | | | |
|---|---|---|---|---|
| $20 | $20 | $20 | $20 | $20 |
| $20 | $20 | $20 | $20 | $20 |
| $20 | $20 | $20 | $20 | $20 |
| $20 | $20 | $20 | $20 | $20 |
| $20 | $20 | $20 | $20 | $20 |
| $20 | $20 | $20 | $20 | $20 |

 # $750 Envelope 

How it works: Each day is $25, take your $25 and place it in a physical envelope then cross off or circle one envelope on this page until you cross or circle all the envelopes.

**Start date:**

| | | | | |
|---|---|---|---|---|
| $25 | $25 | $25 | $25 | $25 |
| $25 | $25 | $25 | $25 | $25 |
| $25 | $25 | $25 | $25 | $25 |
| $25 | $25 | $25 | $25 | $25 |
| $25 | $25 | $25 | $25 | $25 |
| $25 | $25 | $25 | $25 | $25 |

# $900 Envelope



How it works: Each day is $30, take your $30 and place it in a physical envelope then cross off or circle one envelope on this page until you cross or circle all the envelopes.

**Start date:**

| | | | | |
|---|---|---|---|---|
| $30 | $30 | $30 | $30 | $30 |
| $30 | $30 | $30 | $30 | $30 |
| $30 | $30 | $30 | $30 | $30 |
| $30 | $30 | $30 | $30 | $30 |
| $30 | $30 | $30 | $30 | $30 |
| $30 | $30 | $30 | $30 | $30 |

# Envelope Challenge 

How it works: Each day write a dollar amount under an envelope, take your dollar amount and place it in a physical envelope, repeat daily till you have filled out all of the envelopes.

Start date:

$_______   $_______   $_______   $_______   $_______

$_______   $_______   $_______   $_______   $_______

$_______   $_______   $_______   $_______   $_______

$_______   $_______   $_______   $_______   $_______

$_______   $_______   $_______   $_______   $_______

$_______   $_______   $_______   $_______   $_______

$_______

#  Envelope Challenge ✉

How it works: Each day write a dollar amount under an envelope, take your dollar amount and place it in a physical envelope, repeat daily till you have filled out all of the envelopes.

**Start date:**

| | | | | |
|---|---|---|---|---|
| $________ | $________ | $________ | $________ | $________ |
| $________ | $________ | $________ | $________ | $________ |
| $________ | $________ | $________ | $________ | $________ |
| $________ | $________ | $________ | $________ | $________ |
| $________ | $________ | $________ | $________ | $________ |
| $________ | $________ | $________ | $________ | $________ |

$________

# Envelope Challenge

**How it works:** Each day write a dollar amount under an envelope, take your dollar amount and place it in a physical envelope, repeat daily till you have filled out all of the envelopes.

**Start date:**

| | | | | |
|---|---|---|---|---|
| $________ | $________ | $________ | $________ | $________ |
| $________ | $________ | $________ | $________ | $________ |
| $________ | $________ | $________ | $________ | $________ |
| $________ | $________ | $________ | $________ | $________ |
| $________ | $________ | $________ | $________ | $________ |
| $________ | $________ | $________ | $________ | $________ |
| $________ | | | | |

#  Envelope Challenge ✉

**How it works: Each day write a dollar amount under an envelope, take your dollar amount and place it in a physical envelope, repeat daily till you have filled out all of the envelopes.**

**Start date:**

$________   $________   $________   $________   $________

$________   $________   $________   $________   $________

$________   $________   $________   $________   $________

$________   $________   $________   $________   $________

$________   $________   $________   $________   $________

$________   $________   $________   $________   $________

$________

# Envelope Challenge 

How it works: Each day write a dollar amount under an envelope, take your dollar amount and place it in a physical envelope, repeat daily till you have filled out all of the envelopes.

**Start date:**

$_________   $_________   $_________   $_________   $_________

$_________   $_________   $_________   $_________   $_________

$_________   $_________   $_________   $_________   $_________

$_________   $_________   $_________   $_________   $_________

$_________   $_________   $_________   $_________   $_________

$_________   $_________   $_________   $_________   $_________

$_________

#  Envelope Challenge ✉



**How it works: Each day write a dollar amount under an envelope, take your dollar amount and place it in a physical envelope, repeat daily till you have filled out all of the envelopes.**

**Start date:**

| | | | | |
|---|---|---|---|---|
| $________ | $________ | $________ | $________ | $________ |
| $________ | $________ | $________ | $________ | $________ |
| $________ | $________ | $________ | $________ | $________ |
| $________ | $________ | $________ | $________ | $________ |
| $________ | $________ | $________ | $________ | $________ |
| $________ | $________ | $________ | $________ | $________ |
| $________ | | | | |

# Savings Ideas

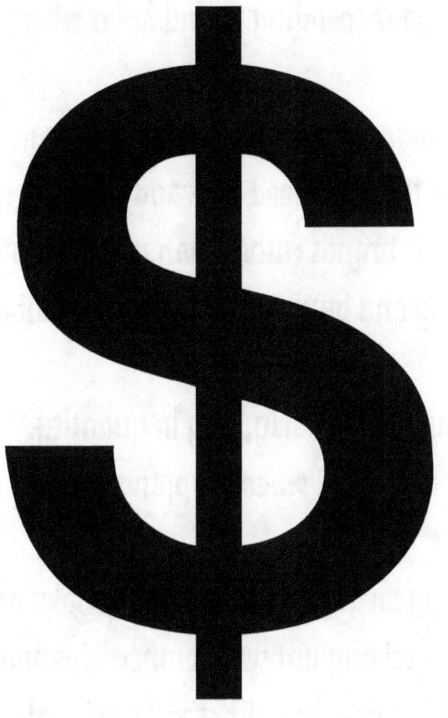

In the following pages are 100 money-saving ideas that you can use to help boost your savings. When you have gone through them, why not add your own to the list!

# Money Saving Ideas

- Set up and stick to a budget.
- Keep a tab on your spending to find areas where you might make savings.
- Make food at home rather than going out to eat.
- Meal planning to reduce food costs and time spent.
- Invest in generic brands rather than name brands.
- When shopping and buying groceries, use cashback apps and coupons.
- For things you use regularly, buy in quantity.
- Make a list and follow it when shopping to avoid impulsive purchases.
- Prior to making large purchases, wait for sales and discounts.
- Refund and cancel any unused memberships and subscriptions.
- Negotiate a better deal on your credit cards' interest rates.
- Pay down loans with high interest rates as soon as you can.
- Look at getting a better interest rate by refinancing your debts.
- To save money on petrol and parking, take public transport.
- For short excursions, use a bike or walk.
- Maintain your vehicle properly to avoid expensive repairs.
- Utilise energy-saving gadgets to lower your utility costs.
- When not in use, unplug equipment and gadgets.
- Adjust the thermostat to a temperature that uses less energy.
- Refinance your loans to get better interest rates.

# Money Saving Ideas

- Unplug devices and appliances when not in use.
- Set your thermostat to a more energy-efficient temperature
- Lower your heating and cooling expenses by insulating your house.
- Shop at thrift stores and clearance sales for clothing.
- Rather than purchasing new clothing, fix old ones.
- Purchase used appliances and furniture.
- You can have a garage sale or sell things you no longer need online.
- Reduce how much you use streaming and cable services.
- Reduce the amount you pay each month by downgrading your mobile plan.
- Buy gadgets and devices on Cyber Monday or Black Friday
- Cancel your gym membership and work out at home instead.
- When feasible, do your own house improvements and repairs.
- Rather than purchasing bottled water, use a reusable water bottle.
- To save money on water and heating, take shorter showers.
- To save energy, replace your lightbulbs with LED ones.
- Avoid paying for mechanics by learning basic auto maintenance.
- Utilize leftovers and plan your meals to cut down on food waste.
- Create your own cleaning supplies at home.
- To control the temperature of your home, use a programmable thermostat.
- Use public libraries to borrow films, books, and other media.
- Purchase gift cards in bulk or as a present.

# Money Saving Ideas

- Buy prescription medications in bulk or generic brands.
- Reduce alcohol and tobacco consumption for health and financial benefits.
- Plan staycations or local getaways instead of expensive vacations.
- Set up automatic transfers to your savings account.
- Pay with cash rather than credit cards when making impulsive purchases.
- Use the ATMs provided by your bank to avoid fees.
- For work or school, pack a lunch.
- Make use of inexpensive or free entertainment choices.
- Grow veggies and herbs in your own garden.
- Lessen your reliance on paper goods.
- Find discounts by shopping all year long for holiday gifts.
- Purchase personal care and toiletry products under the store brand.
- Make unique presents for noteworthy events.
- When non-perishable goods are on sale, buy them in bulk.
- Give friends or relatives access to your subscription services.
- Purchase clothing off-season to receive savings.
- Examine your insurance contracts to see if you may save money.
- Look for free or inexpensive community activities and events.
- Learn how to cut hair at home or do it yourself.
- For babies, use cloth diapers rather than disposable ones.

# Money Saving Ideas

- Make coffee at home by purchasing a programmable coffee machine.
- Home vegetable and fruit gardening projects.
- To make cheap meals and save electricity, use a slow cooker.
- Refrain from purchasing extended goods warranties.
- Establish monetary objectives that encourage you to save.
- For services like internet and insurance, look around and compare costs.
- Purchase and sell goods on websites such as Craigslist and eBay.
- Choose a bank that charges less or no fees.
- Benefit from employer-provided healthcare and retirement plans.
- To reduce the cost and  use of plastic bags, bring reusable shopping bags.
- For higher interest rates, open a high-yield savings account.
- For clothes and shoes, visit outlets or bargain stores.
- Make meals in bulk and freeze them for later use.
- Get rid of  any unused landline telephone services.
- Use water-saving fixtures and seal leaks to cut down on water usage.
- Create your own cleaning supplies with everyday home goods.
- Rather than purchasing bottled water, use a water filter to purify tap water.
- Purchase old books or take out a library loan.
- Use energy-efficient appliances and reduce utility bills.
- Purchase reconditioned electronics.

# Money Saving Ideas

- Choose over-the-counter drugs with store or generic brands.
- Give up costly vices like cigarettes and frequent lattes.
- Rather than paying a sitter, arrange a babysitting trade with friends.
- Pay your invoices on time to avoid incurring late fees.
- Start a "no spend" month or week.
- To save time and gas, combine your errands.
- Ask for a reduced price from the service suppliers.
- If you can't pay off your credit cards each month, don't use them.
- Come to work in a carpool with coworkers or neighbors.
- Instead of subscribing to print publications and newspapers, choose digital versions.
- Rather than purchasing a new bike, fix or maintain your current one.
- Make use of the free community resources available, such as museums and parks.
- Be wary of impulsive online purchases and give yourself a grace period before making a purchase.
- Engage in careful spending and awareness.
- DIY art projects and home décor.
- Purchase gifts well in advance for significant occasions.
- Keep tabs on your spending with a free budgeting software.

# Money Saving Ideas

- Apply the principle of "one in, one out" to all future purchases.
- Make dinners based on what you currently have in your pantry.
- Invest in energy-saving appliances to save money on power.
- Walk or bike for short trips to save on transportation costs.
- Keep your car well-maintained to prevent costly repairs.
- When feasible, switch from using your cell data to public Wi-Fi.
- Use public transportation or carpool to save on gas and parking.